YOUR
A TO Z
SUPER-
PERSONALITY
QUIZ

D1360401

YOUR A TO Z SUPER- PERSONALITY QUIZ

Lucille Warner and Ann Reit

Illustrated by Tom Funk

SCHOLASTIC INC.
New York Toronto London Auckland Sydney

ISBN 0-590-32353-9

Copyright © 1977 Ann Reit and Lucille Schulberg Warner. All rights reserved. Pub-
lished by Scholastic Inc.

12 11 10 9 8   5 6 7 8 9/8 0/9

CONTENTS

A

Assertiveness

Know what assertiveness is? It's being as fair to yourself as you are to other people — recognizing the fact that you have the same rights as anybody else. You're usually assertive when you say "I want" or "I don't want," but there's more to it than that.

Asserting yourself is good practice in becoming an independent person, because you have to start knowing where you're at and who you are before you *can* say "I want" or "I don't want" and really mean it.

Here's an example: Your family is asking you to baby-sit with your younger brother more often than you think they should. You could sulk about that, or even take it out on your baby brother even though it's not his fault. Or you could work out in your own head just how much baby-sitting you think would be fair to yourself and everybody else in the family. Then you could assert yourself.

You could tell your mother you have something to discuss with her, and quietly, firmly, explain how you feel. When you assert yourself that way, your mother will respect you — and you'll respect yourself too. That's what assertiveness is all about. Of course, you may still have an argument over the matter, but try not to lose sight of the basic reasonableness of your position. Your mother, being reasonable also, will be better able to cope with the situation if you remain calm.

Of course, asserting yourself does *not* mean you have *more* rights than the next person. If you're always pushing for what *you* want — at home, at school, out with your friends, on dates — you're not being assertive at all. You're being *selfish*, and that's not fair to anybody.

Answer *Yes* or *No* to the following questions:

1. If you feel you have received an unfair mark in a subject, do you talk to the teacher about it? yes

2. If the waiter brings your hot chocolate cold, do you politely send it back? yes

3. If you feel strongly about a political issue, do you write to your congressperson about it? no

4. If your date ignores you and flirts with someone else, do you let it be known calmly you don't like it? yes

5. If the gang goes for pizza, which you hate,

can you just have a coke and feel comfortable? *yes*

y n 6. If you have to study and your younger sister begs you to play with her, can you say no and not feel guilty? *yes*

n n 7. If you buy a pair of shoes, get them home, and then notice the leather has a deep scratch, do you take them back to the store? *yes*

y y 8. If your parents expect you to baby-sit more than a fair amount of time, do you discuss it with them? *yes*

y y 9. If you run for office in school, do you *really* put on a strong campaign? *no*

y y 10. If your date wants to see a movie you can't bear to see, do you suggest something else? *no*

Score five points for each YES answer.

0-20   You're not quite assertive enough. People *might* take advantage of you.

25-35   Nobody is walking all over you, but do you sometimes find it hard to stand up for yourself?

40-50   Good for you! You know how to be assertive at the right times.

B

Babyish

Here's a big secret. People of all ages sometimes feel babyish. After all, babies are completely looked after. They never have to take responsibility for anything they do. Not many people spank a baby for wetting its diapers. Babies get out of doing things because they don't know there are "things" to do. No wonder every once in a while everyone enjoys feeling like a baby.

No wonder you, too, sometimes can find it appealing to forget you're grown up — or on your way there. When you revert to being babyish, you feel you don't have to pull your weight in the household. Somebody else will make sure your bed's made or the dishes get done. And you can also escape so many other things, like the responsibility of preparing for tests, of getting on with people; you can put up FAO signs — For Adults Only — instead of thinking seriously about litter or pollution or whether your hi-fi is too loud.

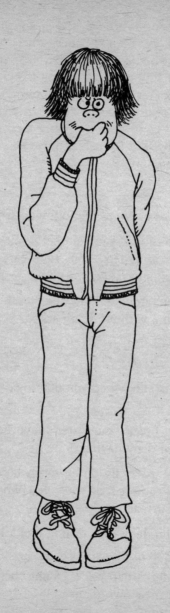

The important thing to keep in mind is the difference between the occasional twinge of feeling like a baby, which is part of every person no matter how old, and acting like a baby for longer than seven and a quarter minutes. What you have to do is recognize the babyish moods when they come upon you but *not* act on them. Being babyish is for babies only and you're not a baby anymore.

Answer *Yes* or *No* to the following questions:

1. Do you think your mother's sole function in life is to feed you, take care of your clothes, and take your phone messages? no

2. Do you rarely walk the dog first thing in the morning without being asked? no

3. Do you feel grown-ups should never be angry at you? no

4. Do you sulk when you don't get your own way? no

5. If you break your sister's favorite record, do you deny having done it? no

6. If you do badly on an exam because you haven't studied, do you give a phony reason for your bad mark? no

7. Do you deny ever feeling like a baby? no

8. Do you feel your parents should always consider what *you're* doing before they make their own plans? no

9. Do you think that being cute is always cute?

10. Do you usually say you can't do something new before you have even tried doing it?

Score five points for each YES answer.

0-10   You're a mature young person who doesn't usually fall into babyish ways.

15-30   You seem to be on your way to maturity, but sometimes you act younger than you are.

35-50   It might be a good idea to try to be more grown up.

C

Curious

Curious can be spelled p-r-y-i-n-g — or it can be spelled bright, alert, interested, and a batch of other things that all mean your mind is growing.

Let's take a look at prying. It's prying when you read the diary your sister hides under the sweaters in her drawer. It's also prying to keep asking questions when your best pal is definitely reluctant to share every detail of last night's date. Prying is intruding on other people's privacy — and it's the kind of curiosity that killed the cat!

But another kind of curiosity is a wonderful quality to have. Finding out about the people and things around you makes the world much more exciting than when you take it all for granted like some old blob. How is newspaper recycled? Why does the little wheel at the pedals make your bicycle move? What's your father really like? Yes, your father. Maybe it would be

fun to press your curiosity button and ask him some questions — about his work, for instance. You may know the *name* of his job, but what does he *do*?

What's the oldest building in your town? If your best friend used to live somewhere else, are you curious about it? Do you ask what it was like? Just your knowing about that place and your friend's life there might make the two of you closer friends than you ever were before. That's one of the kinds of rewards that comes from being curious.

Answer *Yes* or *No* to the following questions:

1. If you read a book you like, do you look for others by the same author? yes

2. When the jeweler says that your watch has 14 jewels, do you ask what that means? yes

3. When your mother is balancing her checkbook, do you ask her how she does it? yes

4. Did you ever ask your favorite teacher why she decided to be a teacher? yes

5. Do you like to listen to candidates' speeches so you know what they stand for, even though you can't vote? no

6. Do you try new foods just to see how they taste? yes

7. Did you ever ask your parents what they felt as newly married people or as new parents? yes

8. Do you watch a variety of TV programs rather than stick to the same ones week after week? no

9. Do you ever read the ingredients listed on a candy bar wrapper to see what you're putting in your stomach? yes

10. Are you interested in doing the quizzes in this book? yes

Score five points for each YES answer.

0-10 You don't seem to be exploring the world very much, and it's worth doing.

15-35 You have a fair amount of the best kind of curiosity. Develop it!

40-50 Great! You're an interested, interesting person.

D

Daring

When you're daring, you're not afraid to risk things. Naturally, that's not the same thing as being foolish. If you dive off the highest board at the swimming pool when you know you're not a very good diver, that's nothing but dumb.

To most people, daring is something athletic like hang-gliding or mountain climbing or swinging on the top beam of the construction next door. Daring *can* be those things — BUT there's another kind of daring that's sometimes just as scary and it has nothing to do with physical ability at all.

You can dare to be *different*. That's important to know. You can dare to like things your friends don't and, the other way around, you can dare *not* to like their favorites. You can dare to openly enjoy listening to classical music even if nobody in your class can spell Mozart. And you can dare *not* to drink wine or beer at a party even if everybody else *is* doing it, or dare *not* to

like pizza even if you and your friends stop by the pizza place every day after school. All of that takes a special, *inside yourself* daring.

It takes daring to dress differently from the crowd, to have different political ideas from your family's, and to decide NOT to be different. *That* sometimes is the most adventurous boldness of all. It goes with remembering that it can be very daring to say "No, thanks" when somebody says "I dare you."

Answer *Yes* or *No* to the following questions:

1. Do you wear your favorite colored pants to a party, when you know everyone else will have on jeans? no

2. Would you be able to politely disagree with a teacher's opinion? yes

3. Do you wear shorts even though you have a big scar on your leg from that time you fell off the skateboard? yes

4. Do you work for a candidate your parents aren't supporting? no

5. Do you try a job you're not positive you can do? yes

6. When you have to do a book report, do you ever select a book that you know is not going to be easy to understand? no

7. Can you refuse to drink at a party, when everyone else is drinking? yes

8. Do you have some friends that aren't popular with the gang? *yes*

9. Can you admit you hate the rock group everyone else loves? *yes*

10. Can you get up in class and say you don't understand a math problem everyone else seems to get? *no*

Score five points for each YES answer.

0-15   You're not very daring, are you?

20-30   You're somewhere in between playing it safe and daring to be different.

35-50   You have the best kind of daring. You dare to be you!

E

Easygoing

Easygoing goes between two opposites.

One of them is getting into a frenzy, one of life's least productive things to do. For instance, the jacket you plan to wear to the party turns out to have a stain on it from the ice cream sundae (extra on the syrup, please) that you spilled last week. Ranting and raving yourself into a frenzy gets you absolutely nowhere. Being easygoing means you shrug a little and figure out something else to wear.

The other opposite is being lethargic. That means not bothering about *anything*. Let's say the wheel on your bicycle is wiggly and you don't stir yourself to fix it. If you don't fix your bike, you might end up falling off it and breaking a leg. That's being lethargic. To be easygoing is to accept that until the bike's in good condition, you walk wherever you go.

Easygoing is being able to take things easy! — not too loose, not too rigid, not too high, not

too low. You'll go along with your pals to the movies when just about everybody wants to go. You won't bother about things that aren't worth bothering about, like not being able to wear that jacket that day. You will bother about things that deserve bothering about, like the bicycle wheel. Being easygoing certainly means bothering when it's a matter of safety or health.

Answer *Yes* or *No* to the following questions:

1. If it rains on the day of the class picnic, do you call a friend and go to the movies? *yes*

2. Do you go bowling with the gang even though you're a rotten bowler? *yes*

3. When you're trying to call a friend, if the line is busy for thirty minutes do you stay calm and just keep trying? *yes*

4. If your parents are unexpectedly out for dinner, can you make do with whatever is in the refrigerator? *yes*

5. If you have a date with somebody new on the same day that there is a real home emergency that forces you to baby-sit, do you invite your date to join you? *yes*

6. If you don't do as well on your biology exam as you thought you would, can you still be cheerful? *yes*

7. Do you smile naturally when you're wearing braces? *yes*

8. When your parents are late for work and grouchy when they rush out, do you yell "good-bye" anyway? _yes_

9. If the record store is out of the album you've been saving for weeks to buy, can you wait patiently until it comes in again? _yes_

10. When your best friend has to break a date at the last minute for a good reason, are you friendly the next time you see each other? _yes_

Score five points for each YES answer.

50-35 You're easy about life and take it as it comes. Good for you!

30-15 Try to be more easygoing. You're on your way.

10-0 You seem to overreact to a lot of things, which makes it tough on you.

F

Feminine

Feminine is a word that's gone through a whole big re-examination in the years since you were born, and now it has a whole new set of meanings. Feminine *used* to stand for cute, and sweet, and submissive, and for a collection of *non*-things — non-aggressive, non-athletic, non-ambitious for personal success, non-competitive. It used to suggest softness in everything, including the brain cells.

Today, usually the adjective feminine refers strictly to the physical: it describes anything that applies to a female of the species.

If you're a female, to be feminine means to be whatever you actually are. If you're a girl and you're the smartest person in your class, that's feminine because you're *you* and you happen to be female. If you're the silliest, same thing for the same reason. If you love sports, that's feminine. If you hate sports and fall all over yourself in gym, *that's* feminine. (If the boy

next to you hates gym, that's masculine.)

When you're a female, to be feminine also means to aim for whatever you really want to do. If your long-range goal is to be married and take care of a house and rear children, that's feminine. If you flip for physics and your goal is to be a physicist, that's feminine. If your goal is to marry, have children, *and* be a physicist, that's feminine too.

Feminine now means all the things in the world that a person who happens to be female can do, can be, can want, can accomplish. That makes it a pretty important word — but it also makes it a word that no longer has much meaning.

Answer *Yes* or *No* to the following questions:

M G

1. Do you feel it is attractive for a girl to be an avid football fan? yes
Y Y

2. Do you feel a girl should be paid the same amount for mowing a lawn as a boy?
Y Y
yes

3. Is it right for a girl to like to do things as well as she possibly can? yes
Y Y

4. Should a girl enjoy her girl friends as much as boyfriends? yes
Y Y

5. Do you feel a girl should be able to make at least simple repairs around the house?
Y N

6. Should a girl let her intelligence show to her dates? yes
Y N

28

7. Should a girl want to be successful at whatever she chooses to do as an adult? *yes*

8. Do you feel a girl should express her own wants and needs to her boyfriend? *yes*

9. Should a girl know how to add, subtract, and multiply well? *yes*

10. Do you feel a girl should try to get what she wants openly, without being coy and cute? *yes*

Score five points for each YES answer.

50-35 You're a real live up-to-date person. No stereotypes in your mind.

30-15 Your feelings about "sex roles" are pretty good, but could be better.

10-0 Your ideas about what's feminine are from the Dark Ages!

G

Gabby

Sometimes people talk and talk and talk and talk and *talk*! That's called being gabby.

There is such a thing as nice gabbiness. That's the social chatter that puts other people at ease. It's friendly, it's light, it's comfortable.

But there are other kinds of gabbiness that work exactly the other way. One of them is nervous-gabby. At a party, maybe, when you don't know many of the kids, you might find yourself giving a monologue when you don't even really want to.

There's talking-out-of-school gabbiness — which has nothing to do with school at all. It means talking carelessly, telling secrets you shouldn't, chattering on about family matters that should stay in the family, gossiping indiscriminately. Very no-no, and other people don't like it, either, even if you think they do.

There are certain kinds of gabbiness that you have to dig deep inside yourself to understand.

One of those is *defensive* gabbiness. Sometimes you can be gabby because you feel that if you keep talking, nobody else can put you down, that you are in control. Another kind of gabbiness that's hard to understand comes out of a feeling that if you're not talking, making noise, nobody will know you're alive.

No matter what makes you talk too much, it's a good idea to listen to yourself and STOP when you sense that you've been chattering too long. Gabbiness can be irritating — and that might mean you are too.

Answer *Yes* or *No* to the following questions:

1. Do you notice people fidgeting or looking blank when you're talking? yes

2. Do you find you're not listening when someone else is talking, because you're waiting for your turn again? no

3. When you're nervous do you just rattle on? no

4. Do you sometimes find you're talking and you're not even aware of it? no

5. Do you gossip a lot? no

6. Have you noticed that people don't tell you things they don't want to get around? yes

7. Do you use the phone more than any of your friends? no

8. When other people are speaking do you constantly interrupt? no

9. Do you keep talking frantically when you think someone is going to say something you don't want to hear? *no*

10. At the movies do you keep talking to whomever you're with? *no*

Score five points for each NO answer.

50-40 You seem to know when to talk and when not to. Be proud of yourself.

35-20 Like millions of other people, you only talk too much sometimes.

15-0 SHH! You should remember that silence is golden.

H

Humorous

A sense of humor is a helpful thing to have. It adds a kind of gaiety and color to life. If you can find something to laugh about when everything seems to be going wrong, that's very good. If your funny bone gets tickled about *yourself* when you've been taking yourself terribly seriously, that's even better. If you have a view of life that lets humor give a balance to everything around you, that's best of all. With a sense of humor, life seems to move a little more smoothly over the bumps and potholes. Everybody feels happier.

But — and this is a very big BUT — there is a kind of humor that's not happy-making, that's *not* good, better, or best. That's the so-called humor that tries for laughs in a way that hurts people mentally or physically.

Tripping somebody is no ha-ha. Neither is making fun of somebody else's problems. Making fun in a way that hurts isn't being humor-

ous. It's being cruel. And cruelty's never funny.

Aside from that kind of no-sense nonsense, having a sense of humor lets you enjoy everything so much more than you would otherwise! It's often the whole difference between day after day after day of DULL and days that aren't dull at all.

Answer *Yes* or *No* to the following questions:

1. If you unintentionally say something funny and a friend laughs, can you laugh too? *yes*

2. If a friend falls off a bike do you see if he/she is hurt, before you joke about it? *yes*

3. If you overhear someone make a funny crack about you that's *true*, can you see the humor of it? *yes*

4. Do you like to laugh? *yes*

5. Do your friends enjoy telling you a joke or a funny incident? *yes*

Score five points for each YES answer.

20-25 You have a real sense of what is humorous. Keep it! It's going to make your whole life easier.

10-15   As you can see, you're right in the mid-dle. Your sense of humor isn't great, but it isn't zilch either.

0-5   You're off balance. Your sense of humor needs adjusting.

I

Immoderate

Close your eyes for a minute and imagine a long line. Color it pitch black at one end and let it get lighter and lighter until it's bright white at the other end. You can see about a million shades of gray between the two ends, can't you? Well, some people looking at that line wouldn't pay any attention at all to the shades of gray. They'd see just the black and white at either end. Those people are the immoderates of this world.

Immoderate people are extremists. They always want things, or do things, or feel things, in a super-strong way. "I HATE it!" or "I LOVE it!" they say. Ice cream is either a quart at one sitting or an absolute *ugh*. The new English teacher is either the most marvelous person who ever existed or the beast of all times. Nothing reasonable, like being home in time for dinner or studying for tomorrow's exam, gets in the way of ringing doorbells for your favorite

charity or candidate or whatever your latest passion happens to be.

Extravagant feelings and actions are sometimes very all right. People are *supposed* to have enthusiasm, and it's not always so simple to figure out how to handle things you're wildly enthusiastic about.

But if you're immoderate in *all* your feelings, you can be pretty confused. If you LOVE yourself today and simply HATE yourself tomorrow, you may never know how you *really* feel about yourself.

Answer *Yes* or *No* to the following questions:

1. Are you either eating everything in sight or on a crash diet? no

2. Is life either wonderful or grizzly? no

3. Do you regularly exhaust yourself bicycling or playing tennis? no

4. Do you get violent crushes on people? no

5. Do you hate yourself most of the time? no

6. Is all your allowance spent the day after you get it? no

7. Do you feel there is only one *right* way to do things? no

8. Do you always feel you're better than most of your friends? no

9. Are you madly in love on Monday and cool to the same person on Friday? no

40

10. Do you have a new best friend every month?   no

Score five points for each NO answer.

50-35 You seem to be a fairly average teenager in the best meaning of the word.

30-20 Simmer down a little! Don't go to quite so many extremes.

15-0 You go overboard. For you there doesn't seem to be any such color as gray!

J

Jealous

Jealousy is not just seeing red when your date looks like *that* at somebody else. It's a dozen other things that maybe you never thought of. You can be jealous of your friends' good looks, clothes, brains, talents, popularity, achievements. You can be jealous of the way your parents treat your brothers and sisters, who seem to get away with things you *never* can. Jealousy, the green-eyed monster, can roar inside you when a teacher spends time *you* want on somebody else.

If you find yourself being jealous of someone every hour on the hour, that's not good! In fact, it's one of the world's most useless occupations because you're *stewing*, you're not *doing*, and that doesn't get you anywhere.

BUT jealousy can be good, too — when it's a once-in-a-while thing. For example: You always thought it was kind of smart not to care about your math grades, as long as you passed.

Then one day the kid across the aisle gets every answer right on the hardest test of the term. You find yourself strongly wishing "the brain" would forget how to count. *Why?*

You're only jealous of people when they have something you want, so maybe you *do* care about your math grades. Maybe you want to do *more* than just pass. That's good to know — and you found it out by recognizing that you were jealous. So, when you get those jealousy pangs, stop and examine what you're really feeling...you might come out ahead.

Answer *Yes* or *No* to the following questions:

1. At dinner, if your father seems more interested in what your sister did that day than what you did, do you want to belt her? *yes*

2. At a party, if your date dances more than once with somebody else, are you sullen? *no*

3. If your opponent wins the tennis match, do you say it was just dumb luck? *no*

4. Do you deliberately snub the richest kid in your class? *no*

5. If a good friend looks particularly great in a bathing suit, do you make sure *not* to say so? *no*

6. If you just *look* at ice cream and get fat and your brother can eat three sundaes and not gain an ounce, do you hate him? *no*

7. Are you glad when the older kid next door gets a scratch on her shiny new car? *no*

8. If you run for a class office and somebody else gets elected, are you uncooperative afterwards? *no*

9. Do you put down cheerleaders, honor students, basketball heroes? *ho*

10. If you're not invited to a party and you wish you were, do you start to gossip about the hostess? *no*

Score five points for each **YES** answer.

(0-15) You're okay — you have the healthy, average amount of jealousy.

20-35 Watch yourself. Borderline. You could slip into being more jealous than you want to be.

40-50 You're going overboard! Turn that energy you're wasting on jealousy into something that's more fun.

K

Kind

For as long as people have been figuring out the meaning of life — and that's at least thousands and thousands of years — the value that always rises to the top of the list is kindness. It sometimes has the name *love*. Doesn't "Love your neighbor" really mean treat your neighbor with kindness?

There is an openness in being kind, a sense of strength, that's like a big warm spirit. But it's not always easy to be kind. After all, how open do you feel, how strong and warm, when you come home from school, say "Hi" to your mother, and get, in return, a bark? You didn't do anything and your mother's mad. Well, when you've got kindness in you, you understand that something's bothering your mother that has nothing to do with you.

When you've got kindness in you, you're kind to yourself too. Think for a minute about how often you can forgive something in others

that you can't forgive in yourself. Like getting a B instead of A in a test might make you hate yourself when you'd never feel the same way about a pal who got a B. How unkind you can be toward yourself!

A good thing about that all-important kind spirit is that when it extends *from* you, it also extends *toward* you.

Answer *Yes* or *No* to the following questions:

1. Do you forget when it's time to walk the dog? *yes - sometimes*

2. If a friend is sick and out of things, do you neglect to call and give the latest news? *no*

3. Are you cold and unpleasant to a date that turns out to be a dud? *no*

4. If you do badly on a test you had really studied for, do you hate yourself for the next week? *no*

5. Do you neglect to talk to a newcomer in school? *no*

6. If you've had some kind of bitter disappointment, do you fail to give yourself a treat? *no*

7. Do you expect your mother to pick up after you? *no*

8. Do you never stop and chat with the old man next door? *no*

9. Do you take advantage of a new, young teacher? *no*

10. Are you impatient with other people's moods? *yes*

Score five points for each YES answer.

0-5   You're lying!

(10-20) You have a great kindness in you and other people must feel it.

25-35 Be careful. You're on the line between kindness and thoughtlessness.

40-50 You don't think of yourself or others with much compassion.

L

Loyal

Loyalty is a kind of cement. It keeps you sticking to the people and things you believe in.

For instance, you're loyal to friends in trouble. That means that even when it's easier not to, you regularly visit your best friend who fell off a skateboard last month and still has a leg in a cast.

You're loyal to friends when they're in the kind of trouble that's NOT physical. Joan's parents are splitting and Joan's miserable and everybody's gossiping. You show your loyalty to Joan by not letting them gossip to you! — and by hanging out with Joan as much as, or more than, you always did.

You're loyal to people you believe in, even when they disappoint you. Your older cousin absolutely promised to take you and your brother with him the next time he went camping. He went. He did NOT take you. But he's the same cousin you've liked and respected

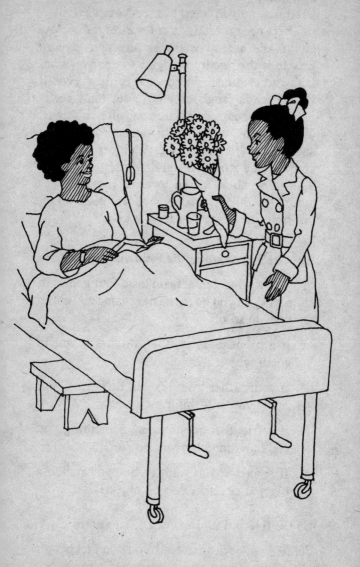

ever since you were old enough to remember anything, so you keep him on your *okay* list.

There are other kinds of loyalties too. A loyalty that's as important as any you give to people is the loyalty you give to your own beliefs and standards. You stick to them even if your friends laugh at you. You don't really believe in cheating or lying, so you don't do it. You would violate your standards if you snatched a belt or a pair of gloves from the counter of a store, so you don't do that either. The thing about being loyal to yourself is as simple as this: It makes you feel good about yourself and *keeps* you feeling good.

Answer *Yes* or *No* to the following questions:

1. When your school team loses four games in a row, do you go to the next game and cheer your head off? yes

2. If a friend is in trouble, do you refuse to gossip about it? yes

3. If your father loses his job, do you let him know you still think he's great? yes

4. If a friend suggests doing something you feel is wrong, can you refuse? yes

5. If someone you want to like you makes a bigoted remark, do you object? yes

Score five points for each YES answer.

25-20 You're the greatest! You don't let people down and people know it.

52

15-10 Sometimes your loyalties are a little shaky.

5-0 Take a good look at yourself. This is an area that could use some improvement.

M

Masculine

Like the word feminine, the word masculine is in the process of throwing off its old stereotyped meanings. It used to be that you'd think of "masculine" and immediately see a picture of somebody always courageous, always protective, forceful and aggressive, someone who never cries, scorns poetry and art, and is supposed to go into the world and earn a living. That someone was almost always a man.

Really, shouldn't *everyone* be able to earn a living? Can *anyone* always be full of courage? Shouldn't all who grieve be allowed to cry?

The real meaning of masculine is anything that applies to a male of the human species. Whatever a male does is masculine. For instance, ballet dancing for males *and* females is a combination of the toughest athletics a person can undertake, plus a special body discipline that's harder to achieve than almost anything in regular athletics. Not even a prizefighter has

stronger muscles or more endurance than a ballet dancer. It doesn't make sense if you consider ballet dancing "feminine" for a girl but "not masculine" for a boy.

If you are male and you dance, that's masculine. If you do *not* dance, that's also masculine. If you are male and any of those adjectives in the stereotype apply to you, that's masculine. If you are male and none of those things describe you — if you're fearful or not very aggressive or a person who really goes for cooking — that's masculine. When you are a male human being, it's masculine to be anything you are and everything you want to be.

Answer *Yes* or *No* to the following questions:

1. Should a boy be able to cook his own supper when his parents aren't around? yes

2. Is it okay for boys to cry if they are hurt or upset? yes

3. If a boy isn't interested in sports should he say so? yes

4. Should a girl be paid the same amount of money for mowing a lawn as a boy? yes

5. Do you think masculinity is many different things? yes

Score five points for each YES answer.

25-20 You're a real live up-to-date person. No stereotypes in your mind.

15-10 Your feelings about "sex roles" are pretty good, but could be better.

5-0 Your ideas about what's masculine are from the Dark Ages!

N

Nearsighted

Wearing glasses has nothing do with a certain kind of nearsightedness. It's the kind that doesn't let you see an inch ahead in time: You don't see the future, even though it's right there in front of your eyes.

When you're nearsighted that way, it means you don't think about keeping your grades up NOW so your school record will be as good as it can be LATER, when you go on in school. It can mean that you go so steady with your "best date" you cut yourself off from meeting lots of other people — including, maybe, someone who'd be an ever better "best date."

Do you have a job after school — maybe sweeping the grocery store on the corner? If you see pushing a broom as "just a job!" and do it in an "I don't care" way, you're being nearsighted. If you look ahead, you'll see that when you do this job well, you'll get a reputation for being dependable. More and better jobs will likely

e your way when you want them.

The long-range view makes sense. If you rush out TODAY to buy every record of a new recording star, you may not have a penny in your jeans TOMORROW, when you decide you don't really like the voice very much after all.

Here's something to remember if you're nearsighted like that. The one thing that never stands still is time. There's always going to be a tomorrow in your life, whether it's really tomorrow or next week or next month or next year. It's always there for you to keep your eye on.

Answer *Yes* or *No* to the following questions:

1. Do you try to keep your grades up each term, with an eye to your future?

2. Do you date different people rather than go steady?

3. Do you budget your money?

4. Do you try to do even minor jobs well, so you're known to be dependable?

5. Do you get enough sleep?

6. Do you watch how much junk food you eat?

7. Have you learned to do a couple of sports fairly well?

8. Do you sometimes think about what you'd like to do as a career?

9. Do you know how to cook?

10. Have you studied first aid?

Score five points for each YES answer.

0-15   Not so good. Try to remind yourself today of tomorrow.

20-35 Pretty good! You usually look ahead, but you slip up here and there.

40-50 You're adult enough to realize that there is always a future and it has to be considered.

O

Orderly

If you were someone you never met before and were standing in your own room this very minute, what would you see? Messiness? Neatness? What would you think about the person whose room you were looking at?

Personal orderliness — in rooms, in clothes, in such things as how you take care of your ice skates and what the desk or table looks like when you're doing your homework — is like a big neon sign. It announces to one and all exactly the kind of self-regard you have.

Too much orderliness is as loud an announcement as too much messiness. If a hair is *never* out of place on your head; if a book is *never* left open; if you toss a crumpled piece of paper at a wastebasket, miss the basket and *never* just let the paper lie there, you might really be tidying away everything that shows you're alive and an individual. Tidying away, or *hiding* away, is not much fun — for you or anyone.

But not to be orderly at all is not good either. For one thing, it says, loud and clear, that you don't care the slightest about anybody in your life. Because the people in your life have to see you and be with you — and you're sort of not pleasing to look at and be with when you're really a mess.

A sense of orderliness lies somewhere between too much and too little. It's that sign saying, "I respect myself and I want you to respect me too."

Answer *Yes* or *No* to the following questions:

1. Do you keep your dresser drawers well organized? *no*

2. Do you remember to go to the dentist twice a year? *yes*

3. If you rip a page in a book do you tape it together? *yes*

4. Are your records stacked in a particular way? *yes*

5. Are your school notes legible and without doodles? *yes*

6. Do you let your mother know when you take the last bar of soap? *yes*

7. If a button comes off a shirt, do you sew it on as soon as possible? *yes*

8. Do you keep a date book and write down all your appointments? *no*

9. Are your book reports ready on time?

10. Do you keep a list of your friends' and relatives' birthdays?

Score five points for each YES answer.

45-50 Is it possible that you are too orderly...too precise? Maybe you could loosen up a little.

25-40 Good for you! You strike a nice balance between being orderly and hanging loose.

0-20 You're overdoing it. Put a little more order in your life.

P

Prejudiced

To be prejudiced is to have an unfavorable opinion or feeling about somebody else for no logical reason. You always form prejudices *before* you have any real knowledge of the thing you're prejudiced about. Look at the word itself. Pre — that means *before*; judice — that means judging. Prejudice is *pre*-judging.

You might be prejudiced against people because of race. You might feel that people are inferior because they happen to have a darker skin than yours, or that people are dangerous because they happen to have a lighter skin than yours.

You might be prejudiced against people because of their religion. That doesn't make sense, of course, because *all* religions ask you to strive toward perfect good. Yours does, and so does *theirs*, those people you're prejudiced against.

You might be prejudiced against people be-

cause of their politics. "All Democrats are Communists." "The only thing Republicans care about is big business."

It's a daily struggle NOT to be prejudiced. That's because usually prejudice runs so deep inside you that you don't even know it's there. But it's something you should *try* to find in yourself — to get hold of and examine. Then you'll probably want to throw it away. If you are prejudiced when you look at the people around you, you're never fair to *yourself*, let alone them. What you do is shut yourself off — from other people, other experiences, other ideas — without any real reason.

Answer *Yes* or *No* to the following questions:

1. Do you have a close friend of a different religion from yours? yes

2. Do you feel it would be okay if a family of another race moved next door? yes

3. Would you try to become friends with any of their children? yes

4. Do you think that all races are equal intellectually? yes

5. If you have a name that associates you with a particular ethnic group, would you never change it? yes

6. If someone said, "All Democrats are Communists," would you disagree? yes

7. If someone said, "All Republicans only

care about big business," would you disagree? *no*

8. Do you feel there is *no* inferior race or religion? *yes*

9. Do you try to be unprejudiced? *yes*

10. Do you feel that *all* kinds of people are equally capable of doing good things and bad things? *yes*

Score five points for each NO answer.

35-50 You seem to have a rather closed mind. Different kinds of people made this country great!

20-30 You are not entirely free of prejudice.

0-15 You're going in the right direction. You usually don't prejudge.

Q

Quick

There are many different ways in which people are quick. The girl who wins the 50-meter race at the track meet is quick in one way. The boy who gets the answer to the math problem almost before your teacher finishes writing it out is quick in another way.

A person who sees somebody wearing sunglasses on a dark day and decides that the glasses are hiding a black eye is quick in a different way. *That* kind of quickness is called quick to jump to conclusions and it's not so good. What if you jump to the conclusion that the tall new redhead in class is "Ugh! Keep Away!" just because he/she smiles as if it hurts. If you took your time about deciding things, maybe you'd realize that a new kid could easily be shy and scared. And your being so quick to decide "no" might annoy you later on, when the redhead finally relaxes and turns out to be *terrific*.

Of course, there are times when it's better NOT to take your time reaching a decision. It's very good to be quick to offer help when it's needed, quick to volunteer for a job that's *got* to be done, quick to take action in emergencies. Those are the very best times to be as quick as you can possibly be. Other times, though, it may be a good idea to remember the famous race between the slow tortoise and the quick hare. Why did the tortoise win?

Answer *Yes* or *No* to the following questions:

1. If a fire starts in a wastebasket, do you *immediately* put it out? yes

2. If volunteers are needed to decorate the gym for a dance, are you among the first to offer help? yes

3. Do you get jokes right away? no/yes

4. Do you like participating in races? yes

5. Do you finish reading an assignment ahead of most of the class? no

Score five points for each YES answer.

0-5   Hurry up! You're going to be left behind.

10-15 You're in the middle. Lots of kids are slower than you, but lots are quicker too.

20-25 Be pleased with yourself. You know when to be quick to do things and when it's better to take your time.

R

Restless

There are two kinds of restlessness, and the easiest to take care of is the one that comes after you've been cooped up all day and want to get out and run as fast as you can.

The other kind of restlessness is more complicated. It's a restlessness that goes on in your head. Do you really and truly know where you're at — and, if you do, are you content being there? If you just don't know, if you just can't decide, if you think "yes" at 3:14 in the afternoon and think "no" half a minute later, chances are you feel lots of things but mostly you feel restless.

Usually that restless feeling makes you want to be doing at least two things at one time. You're having a great time at the movies, but you want to be at the skating rink. You're having a nice cozy evening at home with your family, but you wish you were off with your pals. You're delighted to be exactly the age you are,

but you wish you were grown up already.

That kind of restlessness is mostly good. It shows you're moving, you're changing, you're growing, you're not settled into being exactly where and what you're going to be ten years from now — or even one year.

But restlessness isn't good if it gets in your way. When you can't enjoy *anything* because you think you'd enjoy something else more, you're in a bind. The good side of restlessness is the nice restful feelings you have when you stick to a thing or a person long enough for real enjoyment.

Answer *Yes* or *No* to the following questions:

1. When you are with one friend are you often wishing you were with another?

2. When you're watching TV, are you constantly changing channels or getting something to eat?

3. Do you find it hard to sit through a movie?

4. Do you change your style of clothes every month?

5. Do you rarely finish any project you start?

6. Do you find it hard to make a decision and stick to it?

7. If you're sick and have to stay in bed, do you go stir crazy after a day?

8. Do you decide on a different career for your adult life practically every day?

9. Do you wish you were older one day and a kid again the next?

10. Is a long automobile trip your idea of torture?

Score five points for each NO answer.

40-50 You've got just enough restlessness to show you're moving and growing.

20-35 Be aware of your restlessness and don't let it get out of hand.

0-15 Is all that restlessness getting in your way?

S

Snobbish

Can you look up and down at the same time? If you can — and if what you look up *to* and look down *on* are PEOPLE — then read on! The word that describes that particular trick can be snobbish.

Snobs almost always look up to people for one reason only and look down on people for one reason only.

Some snobs only look at the money people have. Snobs like that admire, and imitate, and try to make friends with, people who wear expensive clothes or live in big houses. Money snobs consider all people *without* a lot of money as "inferior," to be looked down on.

There are social snobs too. This kind of snob is sort of like a money snob, but not exactly. To social snobs, the "superior" people, the ones to look up to, are those who go to certain schools and belong to certain clubs or whose parents have certain occupations. All others are *zilch*, to be looked down on.

There are also intellectual snobs, who judge others solely on intellectual ability and accomplishment. If the nicest kid in the class doesn't happen to get straight A's, intellectual snobs deprive themselves of the pleasure of knowing the nicest kid in the class.

Snobbishness is silliness. It's silly because it's artificial. People *invent* things to be a snob about in order to make themselves feel superior. They are probably snobbish because they don't really feel very good about themselves.

Answer *Yes* or *No* to the following questions:

1. Do you go out of your way to make the richest kid in your class your friend?

2. Do you belong to a club that excludes people because of race or religion?

3. Are you ashamed of your parents because of the way they dress, or because they don't speak right, or something like that?

4. Do you feel that possessions make people superior?

5. If your house or apartment isn't as fancy as some of your friends', do you refuse to invite them to visit you?

6. Do you pick your friends because of their status rather than because you really like them?

7. Would you rather go to a "name" college than one that specializes in the subject that interests you most? *no*

8. If a classmate dresses peculiarly do you discard him/her as a friend? *no*

9. Are you careful to only be seen with the "in" group? *no*

10. Do you imitiate the clothes and manners of kids you feel are part of the "in" group? *no*

Score five points for each YES answer.

40-50 It's time to reexamine your values. Those snobbish ideas of yours are making you lose out on good things.

15-35 Are you a bit of a snob? It's something you should watch.

0-10 You're one of the lucky ones. You're fairly free of snobbishness.

T

Tough

Like just about everything else in life, to be tough can be good and it can be bad.

Good toughness is a kind of inner strength, an inner protective shield. Someone with a supply of good toughness inside is not going to be destroyed by life. For instance, you have a best friend who suddenly isn't your best friend anymore, or even your friend at all. You don't know why. You feel pretty miserable about it. With good tough strength supporting you, you can cope with that situation.

You can cope with criticism too, and face disappointments of many kinds, including bad grades, when you have a good toughness. It even helps you keep your good mood when everyone else seems to be in a bad mood. Good-tough is something you might call the "survivor" quality.

BUT...

Bad-tough is something 100% different.

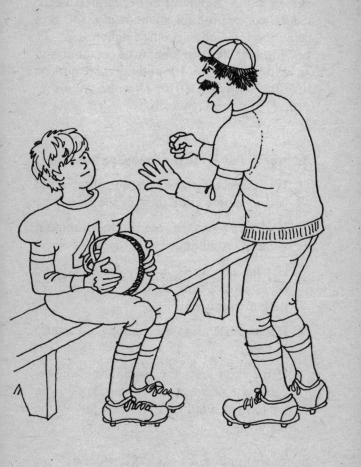

Being bad-tough means to be unfeeling. It makes you unresponsive to *everything*, and that's a quality that's definitely not good. A person with a supply of bad toughness inside has no compassion for anybody else and goes roughshod over other people's right to exist. To be bad-tough like that is not to be endowed with an ability to survive. It's nothing more nor less than the ability to destroy — which means, of course, to destroy yourself.

Answer *Yes* or *No* to the following questions:

1. If your best friend moves out of town, do you try to get close to someone else?

2. If you are criticized, can you think about it without crumbling?

3. If your mother is in a rotten mood and barks at you, can you shrug it off without undue resentment?

4. If a good friend is very unhappy, do you try to help?

5. If the team loses the swimming meet because one person makes a mistake, do you try to keep him/her from being put off the team?

Score five points for each NO answer.

20-25   Tough luck! You don't seem to know the difference between good toughness and bad.

10-15 There is a lot of good toughness in you,
      but some of the bad too.
0-5   You get high points for this one!

U

Unsure

There is no one in the world who does not know what it's like to feel unsure. The things grown-ups are unsure about may be different from the things that unsettle you, but the feeling is the same: "I can't decide what to do!" "I can't do it right." "Should I do this or should I do that?"

Feeling unsure once in a while is only human for *all* people — and that includes your parents, your teachers, the kids down the block, your sisters and brothers, and YOU. In fact, it might be *most* human for you to feel unsure of yourself more often than once in a while. That's because you're still pretty young and there are lots of things happening to you for the first time. Of *course* you're not going to be exactly sure of the way you look or behave or speak or don't speak when you meet your best date's parents for the first time. Of *course* you're going to fuss a lot or stay absolutely, totally, and completely still

when you take your first really long airplane trip by yourself. Of *course* you're going to have special qualms and hesitations the first time you decide to say a firm *no* when everybody else around seems to be saying *yes*. That kind of unsureness is a natural condition.

BUT sometimes being unsure, and doubting yourself so much that you have an impossible time doing *anything* can get in your way. Did you ever hear about the hungry child who could not decide whether to choose the peanut butter sandwich or the tuna fish sandwich and finally just starved to death?

Answer *Yes* or *No* to the following questions:

1. Do you change your clothes a few times before a date? yes

2. Do you never know if a report you've done for school is good or bad? no

3. When you're in a restaurant is it almost impossible for you to decide what you want to eat? yes

4. Are you reluctant to offer an opinion before your friends do? no

5. Is it very hard for you to make plans for a weekend? no

Score five points for each NO answer.

20-25 You're sure not unsure!

10-15 You seem uncertain as often as you are certain. Have more confidence in yourself.

0-5 Put a sign on your mirror saying "I am wonderful." It may help you to raise this score.

V

Versatile

To be versatile means you can turn easily from one activity to another. That sounds simple enough, but actually it's kind of complicated.

For instance, when you're versatile, you can be the most serious writer of poetry at 3:00 in the afternoon and an absolutely carefree roller-skater at 4:30. You can be increasingly independent of your family and also recognize that you enjoy being with them. You can have a great time singing in the school chorus and have just as great a time taking a long walk through the woods alone or with one quiet friend. In other words, a versatile person is someone who is able to explore and enjoy many interests, even some that are exact opposities.

But there's a little danger is being TOO versatile. You may not have to worry about it yet, but keep it in mind if you find yourself constantly involved in a thousand different things. A time comes when even the most versatile

people have to choose what they're going to concentrate on, and that's important. If you can sing well and dance well and play the guitar well and draw well and design clothes well and don't decide which of these talents you want to concentrate on, you may end up being a jack-of-all-arts and a master of none.

Answer *Yes* or *No* to the following questions:

1. You think of yourself as a "creative" person, but do you also participate in sports?

2. Do you enjoy math *and* English?

3. Can you relate to children *and* old people?

4. Do you wear different styles of clothes?

5. Are you interested in exploring stands of political candidates from different parties?

Score five points for each YES answer.

20-25 You're a very all-around person. But better not ignore what interests you most.

10-15 You're not too versatile, but you are able to explore and enjoy some interests.

0-5 You may be uptight about letting yourself enjoy a variety of things. Loosen up!

W

Worried

Most of the time, being *worried* is a question mark that casts a shadow over you: Should you do this? Should you do that? Was that the right decision? Was it the wrong decision? Will it be nice out tomorrow? Did you say the right thing to your date yesterday? Did you look all right? Do you look all right today? Should you have worn the other sweater?

One of the first things that's helpful to know about worrying is that often the things you worry about are totally beyond your control anyway. There's not much point in worrying about what kind of weather it's going to be tomorrow. You can't do anything about it.

The next thing to remember is that lots of times, worrying gets in the way of what you're worrying *about*. If it's "Will I pass the English test?" you can't possibly put your head to work studying when you're using all your energy, imagination, effort, and interest in *worrying*

about it. You may just *not* pass if worrying keeps you from studying.

Another helpful hint about worrying is that sometimes worrying is the smartest thing you can do. If you're at the beach when there are big waves coming in, you're absolutely right to worry about whether you're a good enough swimmer to go beyond the breakers, or if the tide is too strong. There's another word for that kind of sensible worrying. It's called caution.

Answer *Yes* or *No* to the following questions:

1. If you are caught in a rainstorm, are you sure you're going to catch a cold?

2. After a phone conservation with a new date, do you keep going over every word you said?

3. Do you study for exams long past the point where you're really well prepared?

4. When you read an article about some disease, do you watch for the symptoms in yourself for days after?

5. Before a party, do you almost exclusively think about how you'll look?

6. When you make a decision, do you keep analyzing whether it was the "right" one?

7. When you're in a car, do you think a lot about flat tires and running out of gas?

8. If you get one blemish on your face, are you sure you'll have twenty tomorrow?

9. If your date talks to someone else for more than a few minutes, are you sure it's "all over between you"?

10. Are you overly concerned about whether your teachers like you?

Score five points for each YES answer.

0-15   You seem to have just the normal amount of worryitis. Neither too much nor too little.

20-35   You could be a chronic worrier, if you let yourself. But you try to control the tendency.

40-50   You are a worrier. Life will be easier for you if you break the habit.

X

X-Rated

X-rated are all the special things that aren't on any of the other pages in this book. Using hard drugs is X-rated. So is drinking too much. And smoking. It's X-rated to be sexually promiscuous, to play around. Shoplifting, every kind of stealing, *all* lawbreaking is X-rated. Violence is X-rated.

Doing each and every one of these things is a genuine *no*. Doing one or any of them is dumb — not because your parents, and your teachers, and even your government don't want you to do them. It's dumb because they are all self-destructive. When you're young, it's almost impossible to imagine that really terrible things can happen to you. But the fact is, they can.

If you commit a crime, whether it's in a sneaky way or violently, you can land in jail. And going to jail changes you for the rest of your life. If you are silly about sex, you can be responsible for bringing into the world a child

that nobody wants — nobody wants to have, to take care of, to love. Lucky child, huh? And lucky you?

If you want to poison yourself — with hard drugs; with the cigarette drug, nicotine; with too much liquor — you can turn yourself into a zombie. A zombie is a thing that walks around but isn't alive anymore.

If you have the beginning of a brain in your head, you will just stay away from those X-rateds listed in Paragraph One.

Answer *Yes* or *No* to the following questions:

1. Do you smoke excessively? no

2. Have you ever tried *any* hard drug? no

3. Have you ever gotten drunk? no

4. Do you shoplift? no

5. Is pot a regular part of your life? no

6. Have you ever committed any act of vandalism? no

7. Do you consider it okay to cheat on an exam? no

8. Do you enjoy violent movies more than any other kind? no

9. Is there always a green light when it comes to sex? no

10. Is breaking the law a lark to you? no

Score five points for each YES answer.

0-50   If you have answered YES to any of these
       questions, you're being dumb!

Y

Yucky

Yucky means being absolutely impossible to everybody around you — your family, your friends, your schoolmates. It's particularly too bad when you're yucky too often because it's off-putting to the people you really like best in the world.

Going very silent and moody for long stretches of time is yucky. So are things that go along with silence and moodiness: being uncooperative when your cooperation is really needed — to get dinner on the table on time, for instance; being inconsiderate; gazing at yourself in the mirror for a half hour when you were all supposed to be on your way to your grandmother's house almost an hour ago.

It's a yucky characteristic to argue with your friends for the sake of arguing. Equally yucky is to be a know-it-all, no matter how much somebody else might know; or to be a show-off, even if you *are* the best singer, dancer, or actor in the

class. To be sloppy is pretty yucky too.

If you notice, being yucky boils down to acting in ways that bother other people. Of course, sometimes you might want to do just that — bother other people until they almost howl. That may not really be yucky at all; it can be a sort of way to keep from howling yourself. But being yucky as a *permanent* habit isn't helpful — to you or anybody else. It's a way of being one of the world's most unwanted bores.

Answer *Yes* or *No* to the following questions:

1. When you're feeling low, do you often refuse to talk to your family?

2. Do you tend to disagree with everything everyone else says?

3. Do you let others do your share of the work?

4. Do you usually try to get your own way, no matter what other people want?

5. Do you play your radio too high, talk too loud at the movies, or shout on the bus?

6. Do you always feel *you're* right?

7. Do you rarely get anywhere on time?

8. Is your room such a mess, you can barely get through the door?

9. Do you say you'll do something and then flake out?

10. Do you try always to be the center of attention?

Score five points for each YES answer.

40-50 Do you realize that you can be pretty off-putting to people?

20-35 If you don't watch yourself you could slip into the very yucky category. Try to be more considerate.

0-15 There's only a little yuck in you. You must be a nice person to have around.

Z

Zingy

You know what *zingy* means? It means being Assertive in good ways and not being very Babyish. It means being alert with Curiosity and Daring and, yet, being Easygoing in a nice easy way. For women, it means being Feminine. For one and all, it means being just so Gabby and no more, Humorous in a way that makes everybody feel better, and NOT being Immoderate. It also means resisting being Jealous and NOT resisting being Kind and Loyal. For men, it means being Masculine. For all people, whether or not they wear glasses, it means not being Nearsighted. It *can* mean Orderly. It *cannot* mean Prejudiced. It can mean Quick and Restless but cannot mean Snobbish. Sometimes it means Tough. Sometimes it means Unsure. Usually it means Versatile. Once in a while it means Worried. It never *never* means X-rated and hardly ever means Yucky.

In fact, Zingy means all those qualities that

give you enthusiasm and vitality and help you become the interesting, wonderful person you really are!

Answer *Yes* or *No* to the following questions:

1. Do you try new foods? *yes*

2. Do you feel going steady is too limiting? *no*

3. Do you refuse to gossip (most of the time) about your close friends? *yes*

4. Do you have friends who are different from you? *yes*

5. Are you aware of your parents as people, and not just caretakers and providers?

6. Do ideas that are different from yours interest you? *yes*

7. Are you really enthusiastic about at least one subject in school? *yes*

8. Are you willing to bowl or ski or try a new dance, even if you're not great at it? *yes*

9. Do you try to keep your body in decent shape? *yes*

10. The world can be scary, but is it also exciting to you? *yes*

Score five points for each YES answer.

40-50 You're one zingy character and that means swell!

20-35 You're not totally zingy but you're on your way.

0-15 Come on! It's not so hard to be zingy and it's great fun. Try it!